Hacking:

A Complete Practical Guide For Beginners To Learn Ethical Computer Hacking and Security

© By Brian Draper

held against the publisher for any reparation, damages, or monetary loss due to the information herein, either directly or indirectly.

Respective authors own all copyrights not held by the publisher.

The information herein is offered for informational purposes solely, and is universal as so. The presentation of the information is without contract or any type of guarantee assurance.

The trademarks that are used are without any consent, and the publication of the trademark is without permission or backing by the trademark owner. All trademarks and brands within this book are for clarifying purposes only and are the owned by the owners themselves, not affiliated with this document.

Disclaimer and Terms of Use: The Author and Publisher has strived to be as accurate and complete as possible in the creation of this book, notwithstanding the fact that he does not warrant or represent at any time that the contents within are accurate due to the rapidly changing nature of the Internet. While all attempts have been made to verify information provided in this publication, the Author and Publisher assumes no responsibility for errors, omissions, or contrary interpretation of the subject matter herein.

Table of Contents

Introduction

Computer hacking has become a buzz word over the last decade. It was several years ago when computer security was not as strong as it is today. This made for many stories, including the base story for the movie "War Games". In real life, Kevin Mitnick is accredited with hacking into the NORAD database. For those who own computers, we have to be careful with everyday people getting into our personal digital equipment.

Hacking takes many forms. Tools of the hacking trade include Trojans (programs hidden in emails, attached files, and websites), worms (programs designed to propagate themselves through networks), and viruses (programs designed to attach themselves to many file types and continue to propagate). Several other types of hacks are available to malicious programmers and are used by inexperienced people and professionals alike.

In computer forensics (investigative computer analysis for civil and criminal litigation), the most common hack that we work with is key loggers. Key loggers record keystrokes and mouse clicks and send this information to an end user. The end user commonly is looking for passwords and other accesses. With enough information, a key logger hacker can easily move large amounts of money from bank accounts. Often, key loggers are used to watch spouses and business partners.

Hackers are good business for computer investigators. They create problems that are hard to manage; they destroy data, and create access to privileged information, which has further implications. To catch a computer hacker on a personal computer, an investigator connects to the infected computer and begins a series of processes. Much of the work is following the path of the infection from the infection point, through the Internet (commonly), and to the point of origin. A computer forensic expert is commonly used because the work done can be used towards litigation. Forensic examiners can analyze the data sent with an email and trace the location of where it was sent from, and who sent the mail.

Computer Hacking

Computer hacking is defined as any act of accessing a computer or computer network without the owner's permission. In some cases, hacking requires breaching firewalls or password protections to gain access. In other cases, an individual may hack into a computer that has few or no defenses. Even if there are no defenses to "break" through, simply gaining access to a computer and its information qualifies as criminal computer hacking.

The Intent to Hack

To be convicted of computer hacking, it must be proven that the defendant knowingly gained access to a computer with the intent of breaching without permission. Sometimes individuals, particularly young computer-savvy teenagers, break in to a computer or network just to prove that they can. They may brag about their accomplishment afterward, using the stunt to flaunt their computer abilities. Even though there may not have been an intent to steal or defraud from the hacked system, the defendant can still be criminally charged.

Criminal Charges

When an individual is arrested in Florida for hacking, he or she will be charged with a felony. If the defendant accessed a computer system without authorization but did not intend to steal or defraud, he or she will be charged with a third degree felony. If, however, the hacker broke into the system and planned to defraud the owner of money or information, he or she will be charged with a second degree felony. Past computer hacking offenses have included attempts to steal credit card information, social security numbers, or sensitive company or government information.

Penalties for Hacking

Computer hacking is considered a major threat to company integrity, government confidentiality, and personal security. It is therefore prosecuted aggressively in a court of law. Under Florida law, a third degree felony for hacking can result in a maximum 5 year prison sentence and up to $5,000 in fines. For a hacking offense that involves theft or fraudulent activity, the defendant could be penalized with up to 15 years in prison and a $10,000 fine.

Beyond the immediate court ordered penalties, a hacking offense can destroy an individual's personal and professional reputation. He or she may experience trouble applying to colleges, obtaining scholarships, finding a job, or obtaining a loan. Even many years after your conviction, you could still be negatively affected by your felony computer hacking charge.

Computer hacking can also been defined a process of accessing the computer intentionally without any kind of authorization. It modifies the programs on the system in order to accomplish a goal other than the original purpose of the computer. Cracking passwords, extracting important information stored, and decoding files are all part of the computer hacking process. Professionals who master this art are popularly known as hackers.

As the two sides of a coin, hacking also has its own pros and cons. In the present day competitive world, many companies hire hackers as an important part of their technical group to ensure security of their company's key essentials. In the business war there are many who try to extract important information and data of renowned companies through hacking. Therefore, it becomes really significant for companies to hire hackers. Such hackers are true technical buffs and take this job with a desire to master this art and get into the depth of computer technology. Some renowned hackers like Dennis Ritchie, Ken Thompson, and Shawn Fanning made significant contribution to constructive technological advancements. The innovations created by them like the UNIX operating system by Dennis-Ken and Napster by Shawn was a breakthrough in the computer industry. This positive side is truly beneficial to one and all.

On the other hand, computer hacking can be negative in many ways. There are hackers who play fraud and intrigues to various disparaging purposes like breaking security code to access unauthorized network, stealing personal information, altering financial data of a company, stealing significant business information, breaking computer security, extracting bank details of an individual, and enjoying unauthorized access to the system. Hacking can be more destructive if any kind of national security information or confidential government data is exposed. Apart from this there are many destructive activities a hacker can perform for his or her own benefit. This side of hacking is very gloomy and can lead to many computer-related crimes.

There are many ways that can be used to prevent the negative activities of hacking. The first and the most important way is to install an anti virus software that helps in blocking the way of hackers from uploading malicious files onto the system. Avoid using simple passwords for any important data stored on the system or for accessing online bank account. It is always recommended to use a combination of alphabets and numbers that is usually difficult for hackers to figure out. A password involving the name of an individual, name of the company, or any birth date can easily be decoded by hackers. Delete all kind of suspicious emails received through an unknown sender and also avoid using P2P file sharing software.

The Illegality of Computer Hacking

When the Internet became a part of daily life in the late 1990s, there was an influx in computer hacking because it became a big source of personal information. Computer hacking, regardless of the hacker's intent, is highly illegal and may be punishable by fines and jail time.

There are many reasons why people hack into computers. Some do it for the fun, while others do it to steal information and money. Even if an individual does not intend to steal another person's identity or money, the act of hacking itself is illegal, and he or she may be charged accordingly.

Though individuals have become more mindful of computer hacking's prevalence, it still happens with great frequency. An individual may hack a private person's computer or a corporate mainframe to gain information access. These actions are both illegal.

Hacking may take many forms, including:

Planting viruses

Stealing information

Exploiting security systems

Cracking passwords

Impersonating another person

Each of these actions may land an individual in jail. Though this is considered a white collar crime, it is still a serious criminal offense that may damage an individual's reputation in addition to causing him or her to serve time in prison and pay fines.

Individuals who have been accused of committing a crime of computer hacking should know their legal rights. Every individual who faces criminal charges is entitled to a defense lawyer. Having the right defense lawyer can sometimes make all the difference in a case.

It is important for individuals accused of computer hacking to have a defense team that understands the crime and is able to defend the charges with a high level of expertise.

If you or someone you love has been accused of computer hacking, discuss your legal rights and options with the criminal defense attorneys at the Inglis Law Office today.

Computer Hacking Forensics

With IT eqipment and computers so widely used in modern day business, the opportunity for criminal activity to take place increases. As a result of this, more and more companies are looking for help from computer forensics specialists. Computer investigations require a high level of expertise to identify if misuse has taken place and to what extent. One of the most harmful forms of criminal computer activity is hacking, which unfortunately is not just the preserve of movies anymore. Identifying and preventing hacking is essential to safeguarding any business's operations, regardless of size.

Computer forensics can investigate instances where an individual or organisation believes their systems have been the victim of misuse. Specialists will be able to investigate a variety of misuse methods - including hacking attacks - and extract the necessary evidence in order to act in legal proceedings. We can also provide guidance to help prevent future attacks.

Computer hacking is usually undertaken by career criminals who wish to steal personal information and access sensitive company information, using highly sophisticated and difficult to trace techniques. Identifying this is central to a prosecution, which is why we are happy to act as an expert witness in court. We can often present complex and highly technical issues that go into forming a forensic examination and present these in a manner that all parties can understand.

Forensic providers draw on an array of investigative techniques for discovering data present in a computer system, and in the recovery of deleted or relevant files. This is essential to the presentation of evidence in court cases and in employment tribunals. These investigations can not only uncover evidence of hacking, but the theft of intellectual property, electronic fraud, the accessing of inappropriate or illegal websites etc.

A court proceeding can live or die by the quality of the information provided by expert witnesses. The key to providing an effective witness service is the comprehensive training given to those who appear in court. Analysts at digital forensics companies should have undergone thorough tuition that covers the broad spectrum of cross-examination and courtroom presentation. In short, they can ensure that your computer forensics and digital misuse investigations are carried out to the highest standard.

The Effects of Computer Hacking

Computer hacking is a term that is used to refer to the unscrupulous use of technology to obtain illegal access to delicate data that is stored and computer, which obstructs the security and confidentiality of the computer user. It is a method which is employed by a lot of identity thieves to steal valuable personal information. Most hackers focus on hacking personal computer of individuals who are connected online while other's focus their hacking energy into accessing company computers.

How does hacking affect its individual victims? Read on if you want to know more.

1. Hacking is a clear breach of the security of the computer. It renders important user data exposed and risks the user into various threats like identity theft. Various hacking activities are directed mainly towards exposing or stealing confidential user information like social security numbers, credit card numbers, bank account information and individual photographs. These important personal information, when in the hands of computer hackers, can be very vulnerable to illegitimate use and manipulation like that of identity theft's.

2. When your computer is hacked, the criminals may delete valuable information and sensitive data inside your computer. They can deliberately or unwittingly manipulate sensitive data for their own personal gain. This gain can be both financial, as with the cases of credit card identity theft, or medical, like that of medical identity theft.

3. Denial of service attack is another consequence of attacking. This is typically known as the DOS attack, which simply makes various computer resources unavailable to its authorized users. For instance, hackers may change your log in username and password which thereby blocks you totally out of the entire computer system. More often than not, websites are the ones who fell prey to these DOS attacks, which makes the entire website unusable to all its members.

4. Hacking can also lead to theft of essential business information like client's database as well as customer's record can be either lost of maneuvered by computer hacker's. These databases can be sold to identity theft sites where personal information is being posted for sale to other individuals who might otherwise have other purposes for this information.

5. Information that is crucial to national security, confidential government data, data regarding national defense, security and crimes, can be exposed through

computer hacking and these can have very serious consequences to the welfare of the entire society. It can create total panic among the people especially if exaggerated information is posted and issues are blown out of proportion.

These are among the various effects of computer hacking. If you want to keep yourself protected, you need a reliable antivirus program as well as an anti-spyware program. You also need to closely monitor the various programs that you download online as some of them come with a free virus that can be very destructive to your computer.

Hacking is a real threat, just like identity theft. You need to keep yourself protected and secure against any attacks from the outside.

Basic FAQs About Computer Hacking

Computer hacking and identity theft works side by side nowadays. The accessibility and flexibility of the internet has allowed computer hackers to access varied personal data online which are then sold to identity thieves. This has been an on-going business that profits both the hacker and the identity thief at the expense of the victim.

Who are more prone to computer hacking?

The computer systems of small business are the most vulnerable to identity theft. These small business typically do not have large- scale security systems that can protect their database and client information. Computer hackers can easily access customer credit card information and employee payroll files as these data are typically unguarded. Often, these small businesses do not have access logs which keeps track of the date, time and person who accessed there sensitive information. Without this, they will not be able to know if their database or payroll information have been stolen and if it was, these small businesses will have no idea at all.

How does computer hacking take place?

Hacking attacks can be performed in a couple of ways:

1. Hacking computer that have their firewalls disabled or not installed. Hackers also crash on wireless networks that do not have router firewalls enabled or installed.

2. Sending out email attachments that contain keystroke loggers or other malicious software that embeds itself unknowingly on its victims' computers. These programs record every keystroke done by the victims in their computer and send it out when the victims goes online.

3. Attacking individual consumers who use old versions of browsers. These old browsers have certain vulnerability that is being improved with every new editions of said browser. If you use an older browser, chances are, hackers can easily enter your computer because of the browser that you use.

4. Exploiting unsecured wireless networks or secured wireless networks that have very weak or poor password protections. Hackers can easily get inside a wireless network and view what everyone in the network is viewing in their screen. When you enter your personal

information, a hacker on the other end might be recording it to be used for their identity theft activities.

5. Previous employees or trusted users who access their company's computer using their insider knowledge to get inside. These people are often disgruntled when they leave the company so they seek to get even by hacking into the system.

What can i do about computer hacking?

There are a couple of steps that you can do to evade computer hackers and potential identity theft. Here are some tips:

1. Ensure that all the computers in your home or in your office are using the latest firewalls and have anti-virus programs installed on their computers. These programs should be updated as well, or else they will not serve their purpose.

2. Use the latest browser or if you've gone fond of your new one, make sure that you update the patches for your browser.

3. Using your anti-virus program and anti-spyware software, scan your computer regularly for any potential malwares.

4. Be wary about the websites that you open. Do not click on just anything and avoid downloading everything that you see as "free download."

Computer Hacking Protection - A How-To

With the IT era booming, you could hardly find a home without a desktop or laptop. Every moment there has been a revolutionary change in the way we think of leading our life in the era of computer. The advent of the wireless network system has changed the way of life. With the advancement of technology life's becoming more and more exciting indeed! Wireless network systems are pretty appreciated, as it is quite a lot useful, as long as you know how to use it properly. For newbie it can turn out to be a scary nightmare!

Have you ever spared a thought over the security issue? The network security is of high importance; vulnerable security will allow strangers to connect to it and use it in many ways they wish to! Cyber crime involves a lot of unlawful acts such as tracking private and confidential information, spam sending, incorporating hacking code into your website(s) and other illegal acts that might even block of your internet connectivity.

First off... set up a good password - not the just the nick name of your girlfriend or boyfriend, suffixed with a few digits is enough. Set up a password that is not only alfa-numeric but also includes some special characters at a random order. Understand the value of the password, which is a secret key to your network, which should be known to only you and the other people of your network. This will ask people who would try to connect to your network, thereby filter out the people that you don't want to be within your network and from having a free access to internet. This way you can steer clear of unwanted intruders and keep your network safe.

Wi-Fi Protected Access (WPA) encryption is potent than Wired Equivalent Privacy (WEP) encryption. Wired Equivalent Privacy (WEP) can be easily broken and cannot provide 100% security to IEEE 802.11 wireless networks and therefore is a strongly non- recommended algorithm to secure wireless networks. Evidences are there that WEP has been exposed to key attacks many times. It is highly recommended to consider enable Wi-Fi Protected Access encryption, as it effectively prevents unwanted and unrecognized intrusions. For the security purpose the Wi-Fi Protected Access support is built into the latest Service Packs for Windows XP.

I would want you to disable the remote administration which can be seen in most of the WLAN routers. With the remote administration enabled you are exposed to the risk of being victimized by cyber crimes, as anybody can track your network and will be able to get an access to it. I would always suggest you to de-activate the remote administration if you do not require it at all.

Last but not the least, you cannot deny the importance of a potent anti-virus. It is not only important to install the anti-virus to your computer, but also equally important to get it installed on all the computers of your network! In order to prevent virus transfer or transfer of Trojen Horses, worms and spy bots or any other similar programs I would recommend certain names, the worth mentioning of which are Kaspersky, Norton, Nod 32, AVG, Avast etc.

One very important thing that is quite relevant to the current topic is the risk of loading the Share Point List items from an SP lists. If you need to do so you can offload your headache to programs like Blind Share Point List Loader - a really effective program that you can bank upon.

At every single step you might face danger across the web; you cannot stop it! Just use your common sense and be careful.

What to Do If Your Computer Is Hacked

Hacking has been one of the serious dangers posed by the technological developments in the communication industry. The truth is that hacking has been threatening humans from a long time now but due to developments in communications and the dawn of internet, hacking has gain a new life in the form of internet hacking. Internet makes it possible for hacking to reach new heights.

Computer Hacked: What to do

Is your computer hacked? What to do now? The truth is that computer hacking is so dreaded that it can make anybody nervous. The dangers of hacking make it so frightening that it is a nightmare for any computer user. The dangers range from the theft of personal information to the misuse of resources. Imagine an intruder accessing your personal information and using it for his own false objectives. The picture is not so beautiful. Not only individual computer users but even giants are not safe. So what should you do if you're actually made a victim by hackers. Here's a little checklist:

* The first thing you should do is to turn off your computer system. This will give you time to think and get your nerves. This will also save yourcomputer from further damage.

* Backup your important files on an external hard drive to ensure that you do not lose any precious data in case your computer dies.

* The second step is one of the most important of the process. The second step involves the shutting off of all of all your internet connection. This step will cut you off from the hackers reach and protect you from further penetration of the hacker. However, do not think of it as the permanent solution your problem as this will only protect you from hacker's further intrusion but the running processes will continue.

* If your computer is hacked, then now you need to scan your computer with an antivirus software to scan your entire memory and detect infected files. Repair them with your antivirus software or just delete them.

* Some hackers even delete or disable your security programs. If that's the case with you than go for wiping your whole memory. Format your hard drive and reinstall your operating system. This is a painful step but the most effective one. I recommend consulting a professional first.

An Overview on Ethical Hacking

Does the word hacking scare you? Ironically it is hacking but legal hacking that is doing us good. If this is your first article on hacking then surely you will get some potential insight on hacking after reading this. My article gives a simple overview on ethical hackers.

The term ethical hacker came into surface in the late 1970s when the government of United States of America hired groups of experts called 'red teams' to hack its own hardware and software system. Hackers are cyber criminals or online computer criminals that practice illegal hacking. They penetrate into the security system of a computer network to fetch or extract information.

Technology and internet facilitated the birth and growth of network evils like virus, anti-virus, hacking and ethical hacking. Hacking is a practice of modification of a computer hardware and software system. Illegal breaking of a computer system is a criminal offence. Recently a spurt in hacking of computer systems has opened up several courses on ethical hacking.

A 'white hat' hacker is a moral hacker who runs penetration testing and intrusion testing. Ethical hacking is legally hacking a computer system and penetrating into its database. It aims to secure the loopholes and breaches in the cyber-security system of a

company. Legal hacking experts are usually Certified Ethical Hackers who are hired to prevent any potential threat to the computer security system or network. Courses for ethical hacking have become widely popular and many are taking it up as a serious profession. Ethical hacking courses have gathered huge responses all over the world.

The moral hacking experts run several programs to secure the network systems of companies.

* A moral hacker has legal permission to breach the software system or the database of a company. The company that allows a probe into its security system must give a legal consent to the moral hacking school in writing.

* Moral hackers only look into the security issues of the company and aim to secure the breaches in the system.

* The school of moral hackers runs vulnerability assessment to mend loopholes in the internal computer network. They also run software security programs as a preventive measure against illegal hacking

* Legal hacking experts detect security weakness in a system which facilitates the entry for online cyber criminals. They conduct these tests mainly to check if the hardware and software programs are effective enough to prevent any unauthorized entry.

* The moral experts conduct this test by replicating a cyber attack on the network in order to understand how strong it is against any network intrusion.

The vulnerability test must be done on a regular basis or annually. The company must keep a comprehensive record of the findings and checking for further reference in the future.

Know All About Computer Threats and Ethical Hacking

In today's digital world, small, medium and big businesses are facing the biggest threats from hackers. Any computer hacking attack, if successful, can create a lot of problem to networks and in fact all the critical information stored in the various computers within the network. In the field of IT, there is a growing need for professionals having ethical hacking courses to work for them and provide security to their computers and networks. Known as white hat hackers or ethical hackers, these professionals are expert in the area of anti-hacking techniques. They work for preventing the motives of malicious hackers from stealing or damaging important data and ensure the safety and protection of computer systems and networks.

People with ethical hacking trainings work to provide security to IT systems. At times, if required ethical hackers can even break into any other system. But the reason for doing so must be a genuine one for the safety of an organization or company. In fact, both black hat hackers and white hat hackers do the same thing, but the major line of discrimination is that an ethical hacker has altruistic motivations.

There are many major threats and issues related to computer hacking that one must be aware of to understand Information Security in the true sense of the terms. Today there are many some basic threats that you may face as an individual or as an organization such as:

Theft of Passwords
E-mail based Threats
E-mail based Extortion
Launch of Malicious Programmes (Trojans)
Internet Time Theft

Here are some major corporate threats that needs to be handled by professionals having knowledge of ethical hacking and lots more:

Web Defacement
Corporate Espionage
Website based Launch of Malicious Code Cheating and Frauds.
Exchange of Criminal Ideas and Tools
Cyber Harassment
Forged Websites

Not only this, there are some also online threats that need to be also taken care of, such as:

E-mail Spamming

Theft of Software, Electronic Records, Computer Hardware, etc.

Cyber Stalking

E-mail Bombing

Morphing

Denial of Service Attacks

Apart from this, there are some other threats too related to computer hacking such as:

Theft of Information

Email Forgery

Theft of E-Cash, Credit Card Numbers, Online Banking Accounts etc.

Protecting your computer and network can be done by ethical hackers, but as far security is concerned, the first step is to secure the hardware on which all the valuable information is stored and by which it moves across the network. Basically, it means limiting who is able to actually touch the computer, and what a person can do with it if they do gain on-site access. To protect your computers, network, and data from all types of damage and loss that can be done through computer hacking, however physical security can make a lot of difference. Well in physical security, computers must also be properly protected from natural disasters and accidental damage in addition to deliberate acts.

How to Pursue a Career in Ethical Hacking

Ethical hacking is the process of penetrating or intruding in a computer system for the purpose of security testing. Hackers who conduct ethical hacking are hired by companies to conduct penetration testing. These hackers are experts in computer security, as they play a crucial part in ensuring a company's IT system security. If you want to pursue a career in ethical hacking, you have to be knowledgeable in social engineering techniques and you must be able to properly identify the weaknesses and vulnerabilities of IT systems so that necessary measures may be taken to properly secure them.

Ethical hackers must explore different hacking methods to check if a company's IT system can be penetrated using any of these methods. Their job is basically to mimic the actions of a hacker and exhaust all possible hacking options to prevent illegal hacking. Pursuing a career in ethical hacking can be a very rewarding and profitable venture, as ethical hackers are usually paid a lot.

However, before you can become an ethical hacker, you need to have adequate experience and knowledge in networking and programming. You should also have a good grasp of all available operating systems so that you can properly anticipate hacking methods.

If you want to become a licensed ethical hacker, then a course that is related to cyber security and IT is a prerequisite. You should also be knowledgeable about both the software and hardware involved in illegal hacking. Hacking is a serious Internet crime that can be done by anyone who has enough knowledge about how to penetrate a computer system. This knowledge is often always abused to get access to confidential information such as personal information, financial information and other such confidentialities. Illegal hacking is oftentimes used as a tool for theft. Increasing security measures have to be employed to protect computer systems from this heinous crime. A career in ethical hacking is highly profitable because there is an increasing demand for ethical hackers.

Since ethical hacking takes a lot of skill, necessary training is important before you can become licensed as an ethical hacker. You will also have to be trained in the ethical aspect of hacking. As a hacker, you will be able to enter confidential systems that contain hundreds of vital information. Before you can pursue a career in ethical hacking, you will have to be briefed when it comes to the ethical aspect of the business. It takes a certain degree of trust before you can be hired as an ethical hacker so aside from having all the necessary skills, you will also need to earn this trust.

Ethical Hacking Salary - Enough Bucks To Tempt You From The Darkside?

Those who run an online business, or work with computers in some other capacity, are at risk from unscrupulous hackers. But what if you were able to step in and stop them? An ethical hacking salary should certainly be rewarding enough, and demand has never been higher. The fact is, there are a significant number of people who make it their hobby or business to break in to online accounts, or websites, and to alter, steal or remove data.

This practice is known as hacking. Naturally, hacking will be viewed by most as a complete violation of privacy, and not to be accepted in any way, shape or form. However, a good number of people fail to see that there can be good derived out of learning how to hack. Know your enemy springs to mind!

There are many large and small companies looking to hire hackers. After all, who knows better about IT security and vulnerabilities than a seasoned hacker? When hired, their task is to make sure that all of their employers programs and websites remain secure from hacking attempts. They can test the security (by attempting to hack as a would-be attacker,) looking for anything exploitable. If found, they are to report their findings to the appropriate programmer so the issue can be fixed.

There are actually several job openings for hackers in many companies. And with the ethical hacking salary being quite high, it can be very appealing indeed. These people are normally experts in the field of computer security and are well trained to hack into all manner of systems. People with such expertise are very helpful to companies and can potentially save them millions of dollars, much embarrassment and potential lost of reputation.

The ethical hacking salary within most companies is comfortably high (relatively speaking) and rightfully so because as aforementioned, they are saving the company a lot of money, and require specialist skills. There are even training courses available for people who want to be a hacker. Choosing to specialize in this field is quite profitable and can lead to a comfortable lifestyle and stable employment.

People live in a time where we all are becoming more and more dependent on computers. More companies are starting to depend heavily on their computers and any hacking done can cause serious damage. In the near future, ethical hacking jobs will become more common and the ethical hacking salary will be even higher.

Being paid to hack is quite enticing to many for several reasons. It is not just the desirable ethical hacking salary, it is also the challenge the role represents. Further, when you add in the fun factor which hacking clearly has to many, it is not at all hard to imagine why those with the knowledge would go for such a career.

In short, hacking is often seen as a sport by many, and can be outright fun! So why not get paid to do it?

Five Surefire Tips to Protect Your Computers From Hackers

Hacking attacks are constant worry and perennial headache for any network administrator. More interestingly and ironically, the best defense against them comes from hackers themselves. But these hackers are of a different kind and breed - they are 'ethical hackers'.

While companies and government organizations all across the world are spending huge sums on hiring professional network security

experts or ethical computer hackers, you can make your computer secure by being a little more careful and by keeping your system equipped with next generation anti-hacking solutions. Let's see how

1. Always use the latest version of anti-virus software applications. With good anti-virus software, whenever a hacker tries to access your machine you would be warned about it so that you can take necessary steps before any damage is done.

2. Always keep the firewalls in active mode as it will prevent unauthorized entry by the hackers.

3. Keep checking the programs running on your system on a regular basis. In case, you come across some program that you might not have installed or which does not form part of standard operating system, then be alert and cross check it as it might be some sort of spam.

4. To minimize risk against virus attacks and hackers, keep your operating system up to date as it allows the machine to be aware of the latest discovered security holes. If you don't do that, you are just giving open invitation to the hackers who just evolve from every failed or 'taken care of' hacking attack.

5. Never ignore the patches when they arrive for installation. Usually what happens is that a hacker makes a way to enter your computer through some common programs. By installing security fixes and patches you make your computer safe from hackers as they are developed with the sole motive to fix security related issues.

Well, these tips are just the primary precautions to keep your system safe from the hands of hackers. But it's better to take help of experts to take care of security measures. Many companies nowadays employ ethical hackers with knowledge of network security, cracking and hacking to counter the menace of criminal hacking.

Let me explain a little more. Hackers are broadly categorized into three groups:

- Black-hat hacker- These are the malicious or criminal hackers that break into networks or computers, or create computer viruses.

- Grey-hat hacker: These are skilled hackers who have mixed characteristics of white and black-hat hackers. They usually hack for fun or challenge but in the process can do some pretty damaging things.

- White-hat hacker: These are ethical hackers whose task is to provide security and protection to IT systems. Such people are employed by companies to enhance their IT security and keep their network systems free of hackers and spammers.

Ethical hacking is thus fast becoming a chosen career option for young IT pros given the fact that the IT security market worldwide is growing by leaps and bounds. There are various courses available for computer hacking and network security training. Professional cracking tutorials and other courses prepare IT security pros for attractive careers in big organizations.

Key Steps to Lessen Your Chances of Getting Hacked

Having your computer hacked is a disturbing problem for any internet user. It has been estimated that around 75% of all breaches have been the result of external threats. However, it is becoming very difficult to keep your personal details secure due to advanced hacking techniques. Recently, even Google accounts have been easily hacked through cleverly-crafted HTML emails. Online users should be even more careful when using computers at internet café centers (Wi-Fi areas) because advanced hacking software is capable of recording all of your movements.

According to latest web incidents hacking reports, most hackings are carried out using two strategies; SQL injection and cross-sire scripting. As technology grows, hacking techniques are becoming more and more advanced. Hence, it is important to know smart ways in which to secure your personal details with less fear of being hacked.

Here are some key steps that will help lessen the chances of getting hacked:

First and foremost, when you are using computers that are not secure, don't log into email or bank accounts. Instead, use a highly secure personalized computer to perform online transactions.

Next, create a strong password:

Passwords that are simple and taken from a dictionary can be traced more easily by the hackers. Advanced hacking tools are now available to crack the password in no time. So, you need to create passwords that have a minimum of 12 characters and are difficult to trace. Creating your password by combining numbers can also be more powerful than passwords that consist of just characters.

Never type out your password:

"Key logger" is a tool that can record all the keystrokes from an infected computer. So, eliminate typing your password and paste it instead. To do this, type the password onto a notepad and copy and paste when your password is required.

Avoid entering passwords on websites without https:

Unsecure websites have just "http" tags and not "https" in which the "s" stands for secure. If you enter details on websites that are not https, your data might easily be hacked without your knowledge.

IP-address protection:

You can also install IP-address protection software which allows access to the sites you have added to your list. This can prevent unwanted sites or software from obtaining access to your accounts.

Secure your computer:

Enhance the security of your computer by installing high quality antivirus software that is powerful enough to prevent malicious programs from accessing your computer details. Regular updates are a must to update your computer's security from a wide range of virus or Trojans that are created on a regular basis.

These are just some of the important steps to take that will assist you in lessening your chances of getting hacked computers.

Network Support For Computer Network Security Problems

Computer networking was invented to make the computers communicate with each other. Communication between computers is faster and easier than any other mode of communication. In addition to providing faster communication, computer networking empowered the computer users to to access remote programs and databases. Apart from these plus points, there are several other benefits of computer networks. Computer networking reduces the business process expenditure by making hardware and software resources remotely accessible and by downsizing to microcomputer-based networks instead of using mainframes. Accumulating data from multiple resources has become effortless process, which also ensures the reliability of the information.

Definition Of Computer Network

A computer network is defined as an interconnected system in which computers are interlinked to each other for communication purpose so that resources and information could be accessed by all connected nodes.

Menace to Computer Networks

Computer hacking poses a very grave danger to computer networks. This threat is defined by infringement on the secure private information or illegal modification of files, web pages or software stored on computer. Computers are hacked because important and critical data are stored on these machines. One common perception is that all computer hackers are outsiders, who must be prevented from accessing the protected computer networks illegally. But that is not completely true. An evil insider with sinister intention could as dangerous as an outsider is!

The most common form of computer hacking are:-

1. Illegal entry into any protected computer system.
2. Unlawful modification, deletion and access denial to data stored on a computer system.
3. Illegitimate searching and browsing.
4. Unauthorized attempts to breach computer security system.

The objective of illegal entry is access some secret and important data. There could be different forms of such attacks, such as unlawful execution of commands, breaching confidentiality, data deletion and data diddling.

Generally unknown and untrustworthy persons are not allowed to execute commands on a protected machine. When such an act takes place, network security is breached. Such problem could happen either through normal user access or administrator access. A normal user is allowed to perform certain operations on a computer like reading and writing files, sending e mails, etc. A hacker requires that access to perform all those operations. Certain operations could be performed only by system administrators, such as changing configuration settings. Without gaining administrator privilege, a hacker cannot perform this system operation.

There are two types of destructive attacks,namely data diddling and data deletion. Data is manipulated in the data diddling process without the knowledge of the user. The effects of data diddling becomes visible to the user after a log period. I the data deletion process, the critical data is destroyed for ever.

More Info on How To Stop Hacking

There are a number of ways to deter hacking.

1. Acceptable user policies should be clearly established and disseminated to the concerned users.

2. Sufficient backups should be taken periodically. Data backup services are rendered by PC Support providers.

3. The use of filters should be considered to deny access to unauthorized elements. Effective firewalls could be installed with the help of network support providers.

4. The operating system installed on the computer must be updated as and when required. Many PC support providers render support for various operating systems.

5. The security system with single point of failure should be avoided. Any security system that could be easily breached by breaking through any one component is not a good one.

6. It is advisable to take the help of PC Support provider when security is breached. New methods of hacking always keep coming up. It is difficult for a common user to keep abreast of latest means of hacking. Since Network Support providers always keep themselves updated on all the latest developments on hacking, it is prudent to use their services.

Could Your Business Be Hacked?

Computer hacking, hackers, and the unfortunate "hackees" have been a hot topic of late.

First it was the Chinese who were thought to employ an army of hackers to penetrate government infrastructure and the Fortune 500 companies.

Cybersecurity firm Mandiant reported that these hackers were looking to gain access to broad categories of intellectual property, including technology blueprints, proprietary manufacturing processes, test results, business plans, pricing documents, partnership agreements, and emails and contact lists from the leadership of various organizations. The Chinese Government has publicly denied any involvement.

Then a new report surfaced claiming that hackers targeted dozens of computer systems at government agencies across Europe. This was brought about by a recently discovered security flaw in Adobe Systems Inc.'s software.

The report said the targets are believed to include government computers in the Czech Republic, Ireland, Portugal and Romania. A think tank in the United States was also believed to be targeted by the malicious software.

Even companies like Apple indicated their platforms could be susceptible to attacks. They issued a patch recently to fix a flaw in Java Runtime to prevent future problems.

This leads to the question every business owner large and small needs to consider...

"Could my business be hacked, and how I could prevent it from happening?"

The reality is that any business unaware of a potential threat could easily be a victim of a hacking breach.

How? Through a most common technique used by hackers called "Spear Phishing". This is where a hacker will glean names and information about your company from public records which can be easily accessed over the Internet.

When you become targeted a hacker then signs up for a dummy email account. This can be named after your CEO, boss, CFO and/or a fellow worker, sometimes all. Emails then begin to flow from these accounts with language that would be common in the workplace.

The dummy account appears to come from your boss with a different email address. For example if your colleagues are used to seeing email with a person's name followed by the company but instead gets one with a dot Google or dot yahoo after the name then they should pause before opening it.

Instead of opening the email one should contact the sender and ask them if they are using a new account.

Dummy accounts also appear from other sources like credit card companies, PayPal and others. They might say account disabled or something similar. A harmless looking word document or spreadsheet can be included with the emails which can actually contain malicious code.

Verifying the source is a good first step to prevent a hacking attack.

In addition your firm should undergo a security audit. The audit can indicate your readiness to withstand an attack. It can indicate if your anti-virus software is up to date, if a firewall makes sense for your business and should you be employing anti-spyware software.

Software can lose its effectiveness over time as hackers introduce new malicious programs. Therefore it is important to not only install the latest anti-virus software but to make sure it is updated regularly.

Taking preventative measures and understanding all potential threats is a sound strategy to help protect your key information. An IT professional or Virtual CIO can help you start the process to ensure your workplace is safe and secure.

Hack Proof Computers - How to Detect If You've Been Hacked

Computer hacking, just like any other crime, is a serious issue. This illegal activity can lead to loss of crucial business information like client data and significant trade databases. These important data can be either lost or manipulated or copied by computer hackers and thus be used for their own personal profit. Even email addresses can pose significant threats to its users when these are exposed to hackers because these can be used to spam the victims' inbox and hinder their privacy.

Computer hacking is now being conducted side by side with identity theft. These two crimes have joined forces to claim more victims and gain more profit. Being two dangerous forces, they form a very huge threat against the privacy of individuals and businesses alike. Both can have grave consequences like loss of identity, misuse of funds, and even committing crimes without obligation. With the prevalence of both computer hacking and identity theft, one can say that the entire World Wide Web is not a very safe place anymore, no matter how virtual it can be.

There are various information that can be accessed by computer hackers that can pose critical threats to national security like confidential government data and other information that is related to national defense, and other societal issues like crimes. When these information are hacked, they can severe the entire nation and increase the risk of even the government, as a victim of identity theft crimes.

Which computer is prone to computer hacking? Every computer that is connected to the entire system of the World Wide Web is. As long as you have a cable going from your computer to your modem and your modem allows you to go online, there will always be chances that you will be a victim of identity theft crimes. When your computer is hacked, it can be transformed into a "zombie" computer. This simply means that your computer is being run by another individual (the computer hacker), thus even commands from its owner (you) will be ignored. This is very dangerous because in this situation, your personal data can be accessed and saved on the hacker's computer.

Here are some signs which can indicate that your computer has been hacked:

1. Decline in computer performance. You will notice that the amount of space that your files occupy in your computer is either doubles or has made a significant increase although you have not made any downloads or transfer of huge files.

2. Unexplained modification of files. Your files are suddenly modified and when you checked the date when it was modified via properties, it shows a date that you can't remember that you did modify the file

3. Changes in network settings. Of course, computer will try to play with the settings of your network since they will try to gain access to other computers that might be connected to you.

The best way is still the most basic way to protect yourself against these computer hackers and minimize your risk of being victims of identity theft.

How to Prevent Someone Hacking Into Your Website

You would be amazed, (or perhaps not), at how many people want to learn how to hack into your website. There are unscrupulous hackers everywhere and it's important that you learn how you can prevent hackers from getting into your website.

First, it is unlikely that you would be targeted specifically, but you don't want to take chances. Quite simply the effects could include shutting down your website, getting bad publicity, and getting blacklisted from domain hosting companies. Then of course there is the cost to you in time, money and reputation. These are by no means small issues that can cost you big time.

What Can the Ordinary Person Do to Prevent Hacking into Your Site?

The simplest thing you can do is get a very good antivirus and antispyware program installed and keep it running all the time. Be sure you have the best firewall you can get in place as well. Check the list of programs that are currently 'exceptions' and remove them from the exceptions list if you aren't using them or don't use them often.

This antivirus software should be of good quality and one that updates to your pc regularly and doesn't depend on you hunting for updates.

Operating systems, such as Microsoft, are more susceptible to hackers. This is because so many people purchase personal computers that have the Microsoft Windows operating system already installed. Be sure you have the Windows Update set up to continually check for security updates.

All operating systems can get viruses, including MAC and Linux, and can be attacked by hackers so don't get complacent. Operating systems update security as the need is discovered, so be certain yours continually updates for you automatically.

Remove Executable Programs and Change Passwords Frequently

Change your passwords often. This is pretty much self explanatory. A good rule of thumb according to Symantec is to change your passwords every 3-4 months.

Remove any software programs that are executable (.exe) that you aren't using. You can download them to your home computer but if you have any located on your cPanel that hosts your website, if not being used, get rid of them. Once you have a copy on your laptop or pc, you can access them later if needed.

Any folders you have in your cPanel of your website should be password protected.

The bottom line is that most computer hacking can be prevented by having a very good antivirus and antispyware program installed and running. Don't be fooled into getting free antivirus programs. You get what you pay for and once you get hacked, you'll be really sorry.

Take the necessary precautions with routinely changing passwords and protect your cPanel folders. If you have any concerns or suspect your website has been hacked, contact your hosting server support team immediately. Report any suspicious activities both with them and with your antivirus program hosts.

Computer Hacking and Digital Investigation

Computer hacking has become a buzz word over the last decade. It was several years ago when computer security was not as strong as it is today. This made for many stories, including the base story for the movie "War Games". In real life, Kevin Mitnick is accredited with hacking into the NORAD database. For those who own computers, we have to be careful with everyday people getting into our personal digital equipment.

Hacking takes many forms. Tools of the hacking trade include Trojans (programs hidden in emails, attached files, and websites), worms (programs designed to propagate themselves through networks), and viruses (programs designed to attach themselves to many file types and continue to propagate). Several other types of hacks are available to malicious programmers and are used by inexperienced people and professionals alike.

In computer forensics (investigative computer analysis for civil and criminal litigation), the most common hack that we work with is key loggers. Key loggers record keystrokes and mouse clicks and send this information to an end user. The end user commonly is looking for passwords and other accesses. With enough information, a key logger hacker can easily move large amounts of money from bank accounts. Often, key loggers are used to watch spouses and business partners.

Hackers are good business for computer investigators. They create problems that are hard to manage; they destroy data, and create access to privileged information, which has further implications. To catch a computer hacker on a personal computer, an investigator connects to the infected computer and begins a series of processes. Much of the work is following the path of the infection from the infection point, through the Internet (commonly), and to the point of origin. A computer forensic expert is commonly used because the work done can be used towards litigation. Forensic examiners can analyze the data sent with an email and trace the location of where it was sent from, and who sent the mail.

Conclusion

If your computer is hacked, its important to hold your nerves in order to choose the best possible solution for your problem. Hacking is a nuisance. With these simple basic steps, I hope you'll be able to recover from any danger the intruder has posed.

Good luck,
Brian Draper